EXPLORING
THE
SUN

The Rosen Publishing Group's
PowerKids Press™
New York

REBECCA OLIEN

Published in 2007 by The Rosen Publishing Group, Inc.
29 East 21st Street, New York, NY 10010

First Edition

Editors: Melissa Acevedo and Amelie von Zumbusch
Book Design: Ginny Chu

Photo Credits: Cover, p. 14 © John Chumack/Photo Researchers, Inc.; pp. 4, 6 © Detlev Van Ravenswaay/Photo Researchers, Inc.; p. 8 © Lee Cohen/Corbis; p. 10 © Russell Kightley/Photo Researchers, Inc.; p. 12 © Shigemi Numazawa/Atlas Photo Bank/Photo Researchers, Inc.; p. 16 Courtesy NASA/JPL-Caltech; p. 18 © Roger Ressmeyer/Corbis; p. 20 © Markus Botzek/zefa/Corbis.

Library of Congress Cataloging-in-Publication Data

Olien, Rebecca.
  Exploring the sun / Rebecca Olien.— 1st ed.
       p. cm. — (Objects in the sky)
  Includes bibliographical references and index.
  ISBN 1-4042-3464-0 (lib. bdg.) — ISBN 1-4042-2173-5 (pbk.)
  1. Sun—Juvenile literature. I. Title. II. Series.
QB521.5.O45 2007
523.7—dc22

                              2005028074

Manufactured in the United States of America

CONTENTS

Our solar system has eight planets. They are called Mercury, Venus, Earth, Mars, Jupiter, Saturn, Uranus, and Neptune.

4

A Special Star

You can see many stars when you look at the night sky. During the day you can see just one star. This star is called the Sun. The Sun is a ball of gas that sends out light and heat. It is in the center of our **solar system**. Eight **planets** circle the Sun.

The planets closest to the Sun get the most heat and light. Earth is the third planet from the Sun. This is the reason that Earth gets enough light and heat for plants and animals to live. Without the Sun there would be no life on Earth.

Sun

Earth

This picture shows how much larger the Sun is than all the planets in the solar system. The picture does not show how far apart the planets are.

Earth and the Sun

The Sun looks much larger than the other stars in the sky. This is because the Sun is the star closest to Earth. However, it is still very far away. The Sun is about 93 million miles (150 million km) from Earth. If you drove a car through space at 70 miles per hour (113 km/h), it would take 152 years to reach the Sun.

The Sun is much bigger than Earth. Earth measures 7,926 miles (12,756 km) across. The Sun is 865,000 miles (1.4 million km) across. It would take more than 109 Earths lined up side by side to fit across the Sun.

Sometimes the Sun's light is so bright that you need to wear sunglasses to keep your eyes safe from it.

The Sun is both very big and very hot. The **temperature** in the middle of the Sun is about 27 million °F (15 million °C). This heat causes **hydrogen atoms** to move so quickly that they crash together.

When two hydrogen atoms crash into each other hard enough, they come together and form a **helium** atom. They also give off energy. Energy is the power to work or to act. The energy travels out into space in the form of heat and light. We feel the heat and see the light when it reaches Earth.

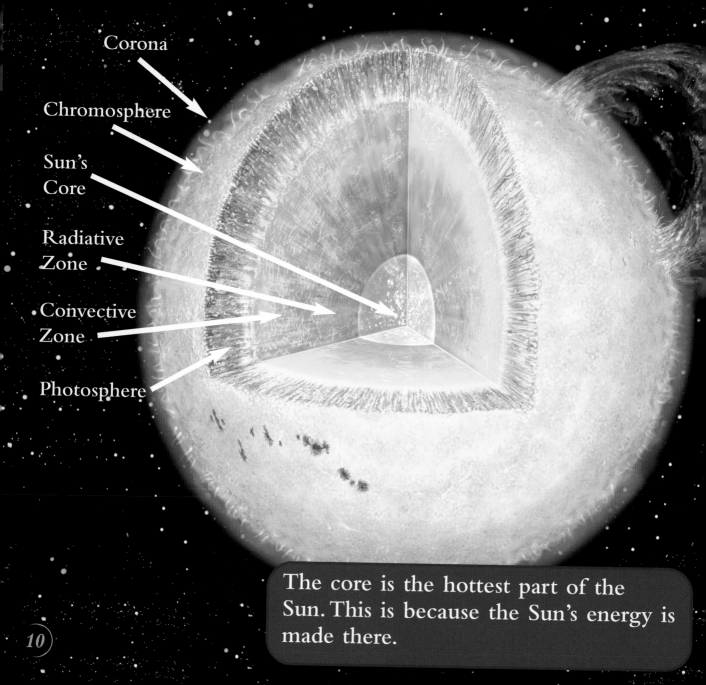

Corona

Chromosphere

Sun's
Core

Radiative
Zone

Convective
Zone

Photosphere

The core is the hottest part of the Sun. This is because the Sun's energy is made there.

The Sun's Layers

The Sun has different **layers**, just as an onion does. The core is in the center of the Sun. It is where the Sun gets its energy. This energy moves from the core through two layers called the **radiative zone** and the **convective zone**. Next the heat enters the Sun's **photosphere**.

After energy leaves the photosphere, it moves through the Sun's **atmosphere**. The **chromosphere** is the atmosphere's inside layer. Its outside layer is the **corona**. The corona is very hot. It reaches about 2 million °F (1.1 million °C).

The right side of Earth is facing the Sun in the picture above. This means that it is day on that side of Earth.

Energy travels through the Sun's layers in waves. It can take these waves one million years to reach the Sun's outside layer. Outside the Sun the waves travel in all directions. It takes light 8 minutes to travel from the Sun to Earth.

The Sun shines on the half of Earth that is facing it. It is day on this part of Earth. It is night on the part of Earth that faces away from the Sun. As Earth turns, different parts of it face the Sun. Day becomes night on the parts of Earth that move away from the Sun.

During a total eclipse, the only part of the Sun you can see is the corona. It forms a ring of light around the Moon.

Solar Eclipses

What if you were outside during the day and the sky suddenly turned as dark as it does at night? This can happen during a solar eclipse. A solar eclipse takes place when the Moon passes in front of the Sun.

Sometimes the Moon blocks only part of the Sun. This is called a partial eclipse. A total eclipse happens when the Sun is totally hidden. A total eclipse can be seen somewhere on Earth about once every year and a half. Solar eclipses last only a short time. The longest total solar eclipse lasted just over 7 minutes.

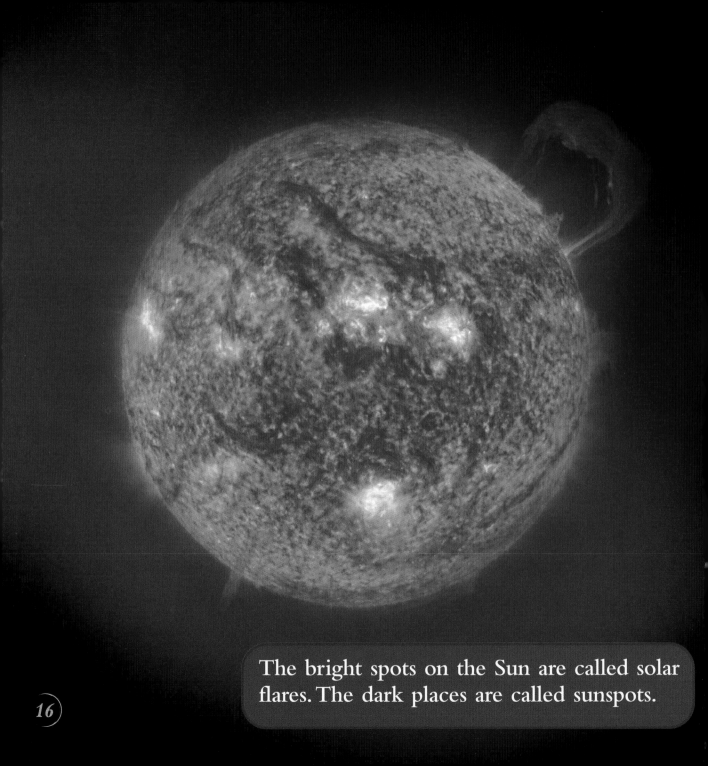

The bright spots on the Sun are called solar flares. The dark places are called sunspots.

Stormy Weather

The Sun causes the weather on Earth. Sunlight warms the water in oceans, lakes, and rivers. The warm water rises and forms clouds that carry rain and snow. This is called the water cycle. The Sun's warmth causes the water cycle.

The Sun has storms much like Earth's, only without rain. The Sun's storms are made of very hot gas. Huge bands of gas the size of 10 Earths rise above the Sun. Particles, or tiny bits of matter, form a solar wind that blows out of the Sun at more than 1 million miles per hour (1.6 million km/h).

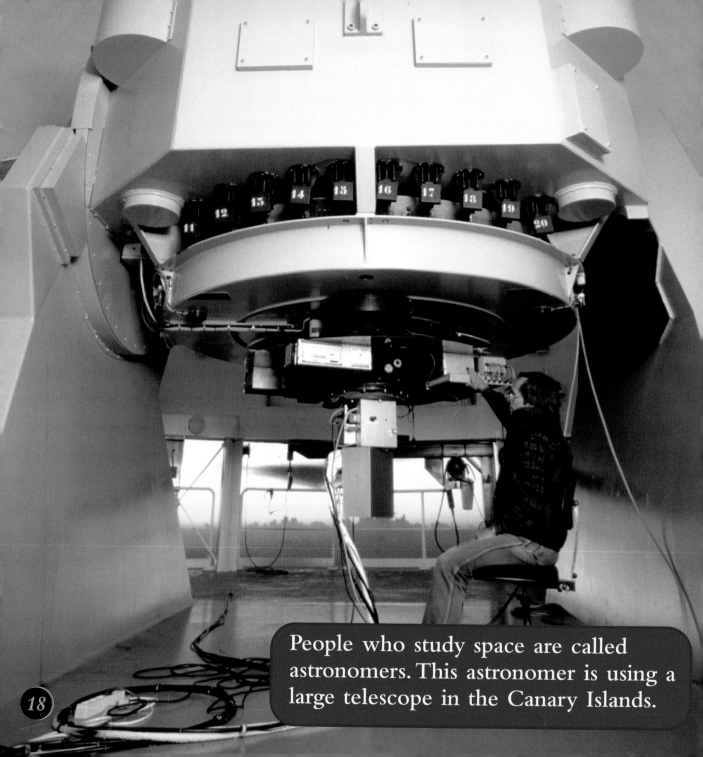

People who study space are called astronomers. This astronomer is using a large telescope in the Canary Islands.

18

How We Learn About the Sun

People learn about the Sun by studying it with special tools. They take pictures of the Sun with solar telescopes. Telescopes are tools that make faraway objects look closer. People look at these pictures instead of looking at the Sun. You can hurt your eyes by looking directly at the Sun.

Satellites are machines sent into space. Some satellites measure the Sun's heat, light, and particles. One satellite found a sound like a beating drum coming from the Sun. The Sun thumps about once every 5 minutes!

The ground squirrel above is
eating grass. Animals that eat plants
form one part of the food chain.

Running on Sunshine

All life on Earth needs the Sun. The Sun gives light to plants. Plants use sunlight to make food using a method called **photosynthesis**. Some animals eat plants. Other animals eat those animals. Plants and animals form a food chain. Food is what gives living things energy.

The Sun also supplies solar energy, which makes some toys and tools work. Solar energy comes directly from the Sun. A solar cell changes sunlight into energy. There are even some cars that run on sunlight.

Shine On

Every day the Sun sends out its energy. We feel its warmth on our skin. Our eyes can see because of its light. The Sun's energy lets plants and animals live on Earth. As long as the Sun shines, Earth will keep getting heat and light.

However, no star can last for all time. The Sun is about five **billion** years old. At the end of its life, it will grow so big it will swallow up Earth. We do not need to worry about this, though. The Sun will keep shining for at least another five billion years.

Glossary

atmosphere (AT-muh-sfeer) The gas around an object in space.

atoms (A-temz) The smallest pieces of matter.

billion (BIL-yun) One thousand millions.

chromosphere (KROH-muh-sfeer) The fifth layer of the Sun.

convective zone (kon-VEK-tiv ZOHN) The third layer of the Sun.

corona (kuh-ROH-nuh) The sixth, or outer, layer of a star or the Sun.

helium (HEE-lee-um) A light, colorless gas.

hydrogen (HY-dreh-jen) A colorless gas that catches fire easily and weighs less than any other known gas.

layers (LAY-erz) Thicknesses of something.

photosphere (FOH-toh-sfeer) The fourth layer of the Sun.

photosynthesis (foh-toh-SIN-thuh-sus) The way in which plants make their own food from sunlight, water, and a gas called carbon dioxide.

planets (PLA-nets) Large objects, such as Earth, that move around the Sun.

radiative zone (RAY-dee-ay-tiv ZOHN) The second layer of the Sun.

solar system (SOH-ler SIS-tem) A group of planets that circles a star.

temperature (TEM-pur-cher) How hot or cold something is.

Index

Web Sites

Due to the changing nature of Internet links, PowerKids Press has developed an online list of Web sites related to the subject of this book. This site is updated regularly. Please use this link to access the list:
www.powerkidslinks.com/oits/explsun